THE BUCKETS

Car Trips and Other Living Hells

by Scott STANTIS

Andrews McMeel Publishing

Kansas City

The Buckets may be viewed on the World Wide Web at:
www.unitedmedia.com

Send Scott Stantis e-mail at:
TheBuckets@aol.com

───── **ATTENTION: SCHOOLS AND BUSINESSES** ─────

Andrews McMeel books are available at quantity discounts with bulk purchase for educational, business, or sales promotional use. For information, please write to: Special Sales Department, Andrews McMeel Publishing, 4520 Main Street, Kansas City, Missouri 64111.

In memory of my mother, L. Irene Stantis,
who always told me it was never too late to get that business degree.
And for my father, George F. Stantis, who assures me that it is.

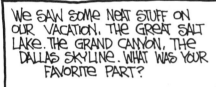

18

29

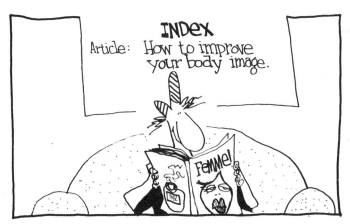

WHIRRRRR

WHIRRRR

Done!

NICE TRY, TOBY, BUT YOU STILL HAVE TO TAKE A BATH.

LOOK ON THE BRIGHT SIDE. AT LEAST HE SPELLED ALL THE WORDS RIGHT...

TOBY, YOU CAN'T RUN AWAY AND LIVE WITH YOUR REAL PARENTS BECAUSE WE ARE YOUR REAL PARENTS! NOW STOP PACKING!...

"...AND YOU STOP HELPING HIM, LARRY!!!"

I KNOW THAT TOO MUCH TV CAN TURN THEM INTO LOBOTOMIZED ZOMBIES, BUT I SAY, WHAT THE HECK, IT'S WORTH A TRY...

HEY, LARRY, REMEMBER THAT GIRL, CINDY, YOU WERE DATING WHEN WE MET?

SORT OF. WHY?

LOOKS LIKE SHE'S GETTING MARRIED.

HMM. THAT'S NICE...

WELL, I'M LATE. BYE.

BYE.

CINDY WAS CRUSHED WHEN I BROKE UP WITH HER. NOW SHE'S GETTING MARRIED. I NEVER THOUGHT SHE'D GET OVER IT THIS FAST...

HOW LONG HAS IT BEEN, LARRY?

OH...ABOUT 12 YEARS.

12 YEARS!?!

I MEAN, THE LEAST SHE COULD HAVE DONE IS BECOME A NUN...

35

40

41

I CAN'T BELIEVE MY DAD IS JUST GOING TO BARGE IN ON US. MAN, THAT'S JUST LIKE HIM!

YOU SURE HAVE SOME HARD FEELINGS TOWARD YOUR FATHER, LARRY. MAYBE THIS VISIT WILL BE A GOOD OPPORTUNITY TO CLEAR THE AIR.

..."OR MAYBE YOU TWO COULD JUST TALK FOOTBALL FOR TWO WEEKS AND LET THINGS FESTER AS USUAL...

YOUR DAD CALLED. HE SAID HE'S NOT COMING FOR A VISIT AFTER ALL...

REALLY? THAT'S...

HE'S MOVING IN.

WHAT?

HE ASKED AND I SAID OK

IF YOU NEED ME I'LL BE WHIMPERING IN THE FETAL POSITION UP IN THE ATTIC...

HOW COULD YOU AGREE TO LET MY FATHER MOVE IN WITH US, SARAH!?!

BECAUSE HE ASKED. HE SAYS HE'LL PAY FOR A ROOM TO BE BUILT ABOVE THE GARAGE.

GEEZ, LARRY, AT LEAST BE HAPPY WE'RE EXPANDING THE HOUSE FOR FREE.

::SIGH:: YEAH, I GUESS...

I CAN'T BELIEVE I'M SELLING MY SOUL FOR A ROOM ADDITION...

...SO GRANDPA'S MOVING IN THIS WEEK, BOYS.

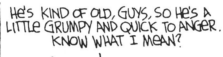

HE'S KIND OF OLD, GUYS, SO HE'S A LITTLE GRUMPY AND QUICK TO ANGER. KNOW WHAT I MEAN?

SURE, DAD.

...HE'S A LOT LIKE YOU.

OF COURSE I'M WORRIED ABOUT MY DAD MOVING IN WITH US!

WHO WANTS HIS PARENT AROUND TELLING HIM THAT EVERYTHING HE DOES IS WRONG AND THAT HE'S JUST A SELFISH, IMMATURE MORON?...

YOU'RE AFRAID YOUR DAD WILL TREAT YOU LIKE A CHILD, HUH?

WELL, YEAH.

...THAT AND THE FACT THAT HE MAY BE RIGHT.

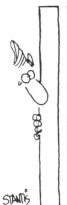

CRACK

YAP YAP

NO, DOGZILLA, DON'T...

LICK LICK YAP YAP YAP

...JUMP.

MAN, I'M GETTING REALLY TIRED OF THESE WHINY GENERATION X'ERS, DAD.

THEY HAVE GOOFY HAIR, WEIRD CLOTHES AND THEY COP THIS ATTITUDE THAT JUST SCREAMS...

"I'M YOUNGER THAN YOU"?

THAT'S IT! AND IT REALLY TICKS ME OFF, TOO...

56

GEL? WHAT GEL? I HAVEN'T SEEN ANY GEL...

GEEZ, YOU BLAME ME FOR EVERYTHING!!!

YOU KNOW YOU'RE A PARENT WHEN...

..YOU CAN'T REMEMBER WHAT HOT FOOD IS LIKE.

YOU KNOW YOU'RE A PARENT WHEN...

HMM... SCOOBY DOO... IT MUST BE FOUR O'CLOCK...

YOU CAN TELL TIME BY WHAT'S ON THE CARTOON NETWORK...

THE PINEWOOD RACER RACE WAS SO HUMILIATING! ALL THESE DADS MADE THESE HIGH-TECH CARS!

THEY ALL LOOKED DOWN ON OUR CRUMMY CAR! SO WE DID THE ONLY THING WE COULD...

WE WON!

THE KIDS HAVE BEEN DRIVING ME NUTS LATELY, DAD!

SO DO WHAT I DID.

WHAT ARE YOU TALKING ABOUT? YOU WERE NEVER AROUND!!!

WE DON'T GIVE YOUR GENERATION NEARLY ENOUGH RESPECT...

EDDIE LIKES TO MAKE A BOLD FASHION STATEMENT...

...TODAY HE SEEMS TO BE SAYING "YEECH."

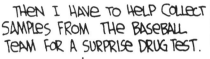

AWWWWWWW! MOM! DOGZILLA LICKED MY FACE OFF!!

ARE THOSE MY NEW PANTY HOSE!?! HOW DID THEY GET ALL WET?!? THEY'RE RUINED!!!!!!

MOMS JUST DON'T GET IT...

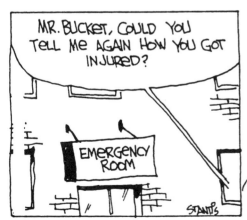

DAD'S GOING TO BE OK. HE JUST GOT A FEW STITCHES FROM HIS KONK ON THE HEAD.

HE'S FINE AND NOT IN ANY DANGER...

...SO TAKE DOWN THE YARD SALE SIGNS AND PUT DAD'S STUFF BACK IN THE HOUSE!!!

HERE'S SOMETHING FOR YOU FROM A HIGH SCHOOL REUNION COMMITTEE.

GEE, ALREADY? WHICH ONE IS IT? 25? 30?

50!!!

SIGH
HOW DID IT GET SO LATE SO SOON?

I GOT THIS INVITATION TO MY 50TH HIGH SCHOOL REUNION, LARRY. I WAS WONDERING IF YOU'D LIKE TO GO WITH ME.

GEORGE CHAMBERS IS GOING TO BE THERE AND I REALLY WANT YOU THERE.

YOU WANT TO SHOW ME OFF? THAT'S REALLY NICE, DAD.

ACTUALLY, GEORGE BEAT ME UP IN 11TH GRADE AND I WANT YOU TO HOLD HIM SO I CAN RETURN THE FAVOR!!!

♪ GONNA TAKE A SENTIMENTAL JOURNEY...

STANTIS

I DON'T KNOW. HE'S HAD THAT LOOK ON HIS FACE EVER SINCE HIS CLASS REUNION.

I WAS THINKING OF PUTTING A CEILING FAN UP HERE.

I MEAN, HOW HARD COULD THAT BE?

WHY DO I HAVE THIS HORRIBLE FEELING I KNOW THE ANSWER TO THAT?

SO, YOU'RE PUTTING UP A CEILING FAN, EH, SON?

B-ZAP

STANTIS

WISH I COULD SAY THIS SURPRISES ME...

DON'T YOU HAVE TO GO MENTALLY SCAR THE GRANDKIDS ABOUT NOW?

77

79

SOMETIMES WHEN I'M DRIVING TO WORK I THINK ABOUT MY FAMILY

AND A SMILE ALWAYS COMES TO MY FACE AS I WONDER...

...HOW FAR COULD I GET BEFORE THEY NOTICED I WAS GONE?

ALL I'M SAYING IS I WISH WE HAD A PLAN FOR PAYING FOR THE BOYS' COLLEGE THAT DIDN'T REQUIRE MATCHING SIX NUMBERS...

LOTTERY TICKETS SOLD HERE

ARRGHH

GEEZ, MY DAD REALLY KNOWS HOW TO PUSH MY BUTTONS!!!

OF COURSE HE DOES. HE'S THE ONE WHO INSTALLED THEM.

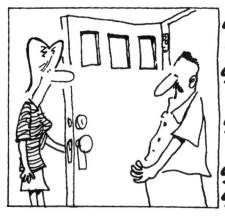

SARAH'S HAVING A ROUGH TIME WITH THE KIDS THIS SUMMER VACATION. ANY ADVICE, DAD?

WORK LATE AND TAKE THE LONG WAY HOME. DON'T WALK THROUGH THE DOOR ANY SOONER THAN YOU HAVE TO, SON

I MEANT FOR HER!

OH, RIGHT. THIS IS THE '90s, HUH?

CAN WE GET THIS? CAN WE? CAN WE? CAN WE?

COMPUTERVILLE

DOOM II? GEE, I DON'T KNOW...

PLEEEEASE? PLEASE, OH, PLEASE OH, PLEASE!?!

OH, OK...

GOODY! GOODY! GOODY!

HEY. WE'RE HOME FROM SCHOOL!

DOOM II AGAIN? YOU WERE PLAYING THIS WHEN THE KIDS AND I LEFT THIS MORNING...

OH, WELL, WE'RE GLAD YOU'RE HOME EARLY FROM WORK...

WORK?

PENNY FOR YOUR THOUGHTS.

I WAS JUST THINKING IT MIGHT BE NICE TO HAVE ANOTHER BABY.

THAT'S WHAT'S SCARY ABOUT CRAZY PEOPLE... THEY LOOK JUST LIKE THE REST OF US...

TOBY!

RRRRRRRR

RRRRRRRR

RRRRRRRR

TOBY! LEAVE THE BUTTONS ON MY SEAT ALONE!!!

I CAN'T CLEAN UP MY ROOM! I GLUED ALL MY STUFF TO THE FLOOR...

THIS IS MY MOM'S FILE CABINET...

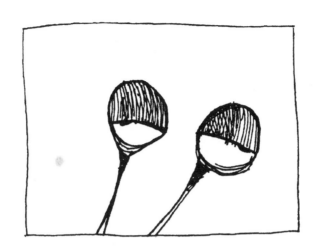

THEY LIVE IN DARK, DANK PLACES...

WALLOWING IN INDESCRIBABLE MUCK FOR INTERMINABLE LENGTHS OF TIME...

AND LEAVING DISGUSTING TRAILS...

DITTO

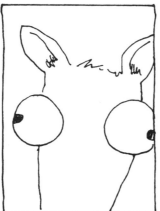

LET ME GUESS...

...YOU WANT TO GO OUT.

WHO PUT WITE-OUT ON EVERY PHOTO OF YOUR BROTHER?

I HATE RAKING LEAVES. BUT I THINK I'VE FOUND A SOLUTION.

I DECIDED TO TAKE A PAGE FROM NATURE...

SO I BOUGHT A BLOWER AND NOW THEY'RE THE NEIGHBORS' PROBLEM.

PHONOPHOBIA: THE FEAR THAT YOU WON'T ANSWER THE CORDLESS PHONE BEFORE THE CALLER IS ROLLED OVER TO VOICE MAIL...

BReeeeee

WHEN I WAS YOUR AGE, THEY USED TO BURN LEAVES IN THE FALL

COOL!

AFTER THEY FELL OFF THE TREE...

RATS!

I'M THIRSTY!

YAP YAP YAP

Z

?

THERE ARE TIMES WHEN PARENTS NEED TO KNOW WHAT THEIR CHILD IS UP TO. THIS ISN'T ONE OF THEM...

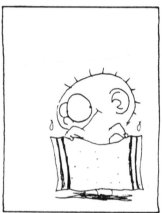

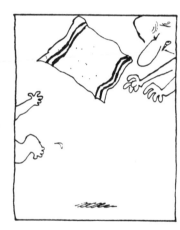

NO, REALLY, THAT WASN'T OUR CHILD. WE'VE NEVER SEEN HIM BEFORE!

YOU HAVE TO SAY SOMETHING BEFORE YOU THROW A BASEBALL, EDDIE...

...NOW GO APOLOGIZE TO GRANDPA.

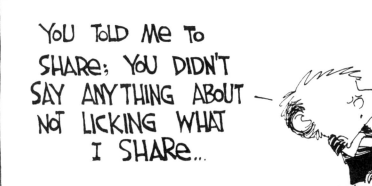

THE DENTIST WILL SEE YOU NOW...

HER! HER! TAKE HER!!!

ACTUALLY, MS. CASEY IS THE ONE I WAS TALKING TO...

I KNEW THAT! IT WAS A JOKE... HEE-HEE.

HEY, WHAT'S THIS DO?

BIZZZZZZ

Weeeeee

NURSE, GET THE MASK. WE'RE GOING TO HAVE TO GAS MR. BUCKET AGAIN...

HI DOCTOR...

BZZZZZZZZZ

ZZZZZZZZZ

ZZZZZZZZ

OH, FOR PETE'S SAKE, LARRY, I HAVEN'T EVEN PUT THE DRILL IN YOUR MOUTH. GEEZ!

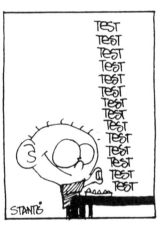

117

CAN'T WE DISCUSS THIS LIKE ONE INTELLIGENT HUMAN BEING AND HER HUSBAND?

IF YOU THINK THAT'S BAD, MY TEACHER'S BEING HELD BACK...

REPORT CARD

I'M ALL IN FAVOR OF QUALITY TIME, BUT DO WE HAVE TO SPEND IT TOGETHER?

YAP YAP

"...AND ON CHRISTMAS EVE, SANTA COMES DOWN THE CHIMNEY WITH PRESENTS!"

HEY! WHO PUT ALL OF THESE PILLOWS IN THE FIRE-PLACE?!?

YOU KNOW, EDDIE, CHRISTMAS ISN'T JUST ABOUT PRESENTS...

SOMETIMES I THINK PEOPLE HAVE FORGOTTEN WHO IT'S ABOUT...

— YEAH!

SANTA!!!

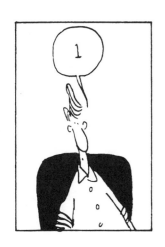

1

1

1!

1!!

CHRISTMAS IS ONE DAY AWAY!! NOW STOP ASKING!!!

127